UNDER THE SEA

Conceived and created
by Claude Delafosse
and Gallimard Jeunesse
Illustrated by
Pierre de Hugo

HIDDEN WORLD

A FIRST DISCOVERY BOOK

SCHOLASTIC INC.

New York   Toronto   London   Auckland   Sydney

It is very dark at the bottom of the deep sea. It is very hard to see all the incredible things that live there.

With this book, you will be able to discover the secrets of the deepest oceans, almost as though you could dive there yourself.

With a simple paper flashlight, the world of the oceans will be revealed as you explore the pages of this book.

Remove the paper flashlight from the back of the book. Move the flashlight between the black pages and the plastic pages to discover hidden images.

When you look out at the ocean
you might see
a boat, some waves,
and perhaps a fish
or two.

But when you dive beneath the waves, you will discover a world full of incredible landscapes and colorful fish. In order to find the secrets beneath the sea, take your flashlight so that you can see more clearly.

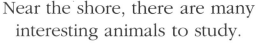

Near the shore, there are many interesting animals to study.

The jellyfish is moved by the currents.

Sea anemones look a bit like flowers.

Sea urchins are covered in spines.

The crab looks funny when it walks sideways.

The hermit crab lives inside an empty shell it has found.

The starfish has five arms.

The mussel attaches itself to rocks.

The sponge is a colony of animals that resembles a plant.

The shrimp has eyes on the ends of two short stalks.

A little further out, you find the sea animals
that live in deeper water.

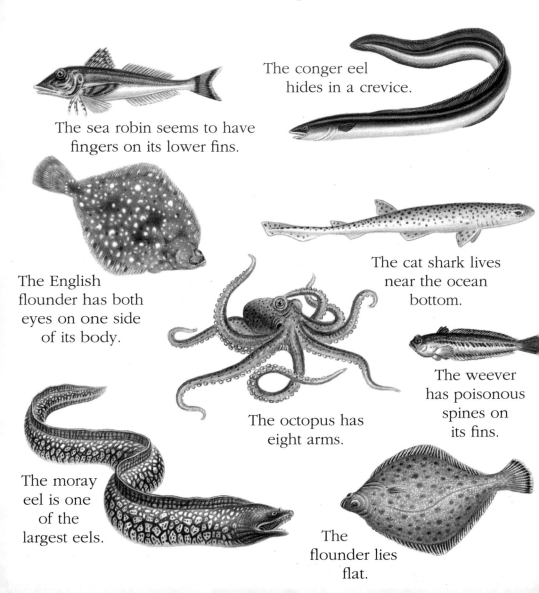

The conger eel
hides in a crevice.

The sea robin seems to have
fingers on its lower fins.

The cat shark lives
near the ocean
bottom.

The English
flounder has both
eyes on one side
of its body.

The weever
has poisonous
spines on
its fins.

The octopus has
eight arms.

The moray
eel is one
of the
largest eels.

The
flounder lies
flat.

Even further out, in the open sea,
you will find other fish.

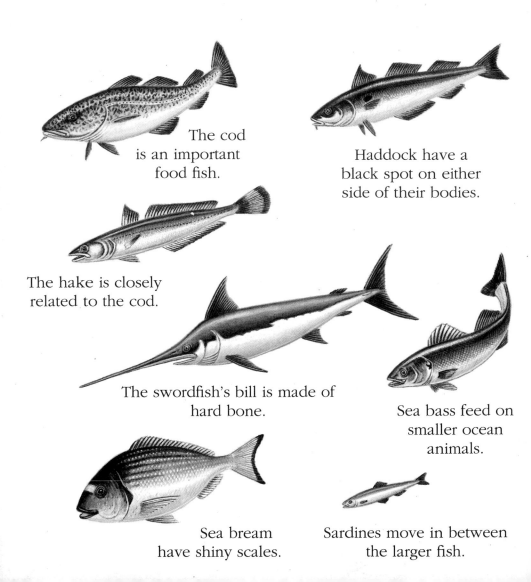

The cod
is an important
food fish.

Haddock have a
black spot on either
side of their bodies.

The hake is closely
related to the cod.

The swordfish's bill is made of
hard bone.

Sea bass feed on
smaller ocean
animals.

Sea bream
have shiny scales.

Sardines move in between
the larger fish.

Way out in the open sea live
the largest of the sea animals.

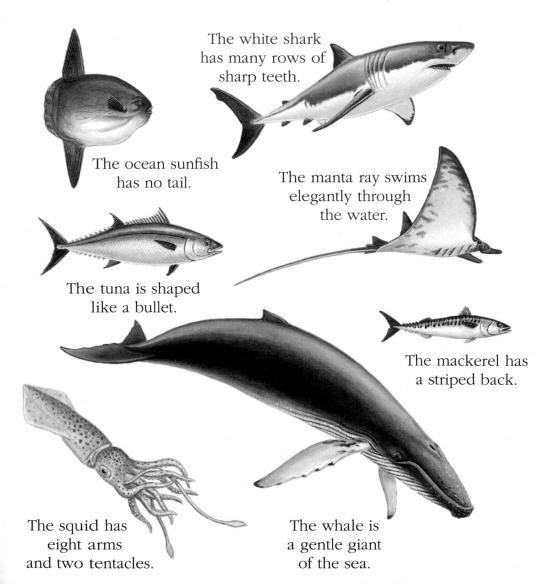

The white shark
has many rows of
sharp teeth.

The ocean sunfish
has no tail.

The manta ray swims
elegantly through
the water.

The tuna is shaped
like a bullet.

The mackerel has
a striped back.

The squid has
eight arms
and two tentacles.

The whale is
a gentle giant
of the sea.

In the deepest waters, you will find
some very strange sea creatures.

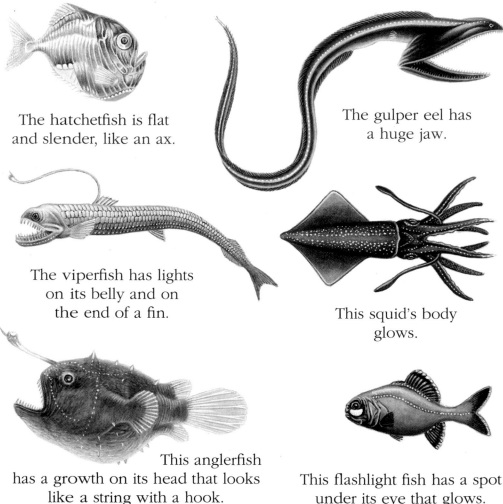

The hatchetfish is flat
and slender, like an ax.

The gulper eel has
a huge jaw.

The viperfish has lights
on its belly and on
the end of a fin.

This squid's body
glows.

This anglerfish
has a growth on its head that looks
like a string with a hook.

This flashlight fish has a spot
under its eye that glows.

Coral reefs have many beautifully colored fish.

The mandarin fish looks like an exotic painting.

The angelfish has brilliant stripes.

The sea horse uses fins on its back to travel quickly.

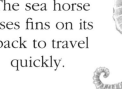

The butterfly fish has a spot on its back that looks like an eye, to fool its enemies.

The surgeonfish has two sharp points on its tail.

The clownfish hides in a sea anemone when there is danger.

To explore while under the sea,
you need a mask, fins, and a
snorkel.

To go deeper under the sea,
you need an air tank.

It is also possible to stay under the sea
in a research submarine, an underwater ship
built for deep water.

You can also dive deep
into the ocean with a
special air tank that is
connected to the surface
by an air hose.

Did you find these hidden images...

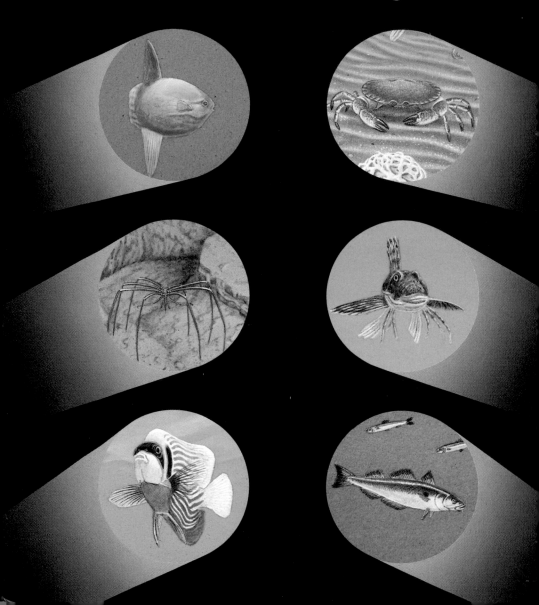

Library of Congress Cataloging-in-Publication Data available.

Originally published in France in 1997 under the title *J'Observe: les poissons* by Editions Gallimard Jeunesse.
No part of this publication may be reproduced, or stored in a retrieval system, or transmitted in any form or by
any means, electronic, mechanical, photocopying, recording, or otherwise, without written permission of the
publisher. For information regarding permission, write to Scholastic Inc., Attention: Permissions Department,
555 Broadway, New York, NY 10012.
ISBN 0-590-10992-8
Copyright © 1997 by Editions Gallimard Jeunesse.
This edition English translation by Wendy Barish. Copyright © 1999 by Scholastic Inc.
This edition American text by Mary Varilla. Copyright © 1999 by Scholastic Inc.
This edition Expert Reader: Karsten Hartel, Curatorial Associate in Icthyology,
Museum of Comparative Zoology, Harvard University
All rights reserved. First published in the U.S.A. in 1999 by Scholastic Inc.
by arrangement with Editions Gallimard Jeunesse, 5 rue Sebastien-Bottin, F-75007, Paris, France.
SCHOLASTIC and A FIRST DISCOVERY BOOK and associated logos are trademarks
and/or registered trademarks of Scholastic Inc.
10 9 8 7 6 5 4 3 2 1   9/9 0/0 01 02 03 04
Printed in Italy by Editoriale Libraria.
First Scholastic printing, March, 1999.